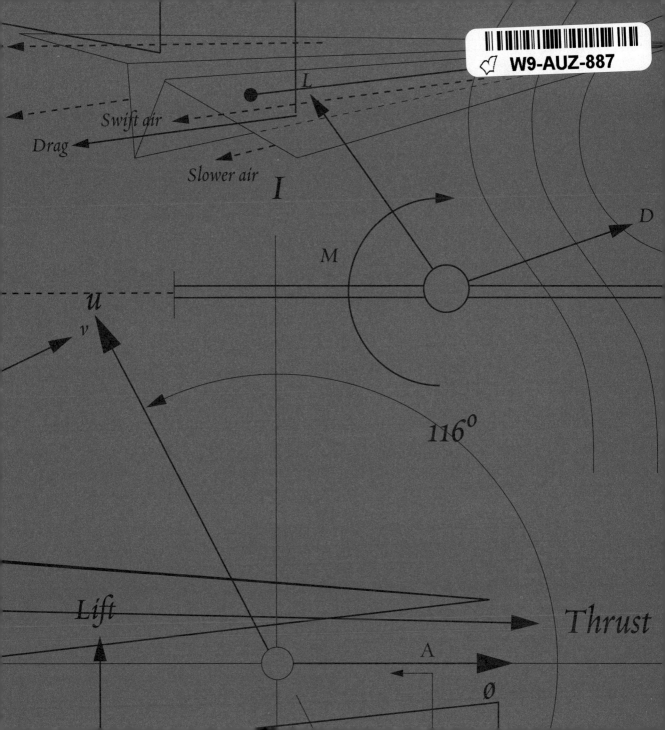

W9-AUZ-887

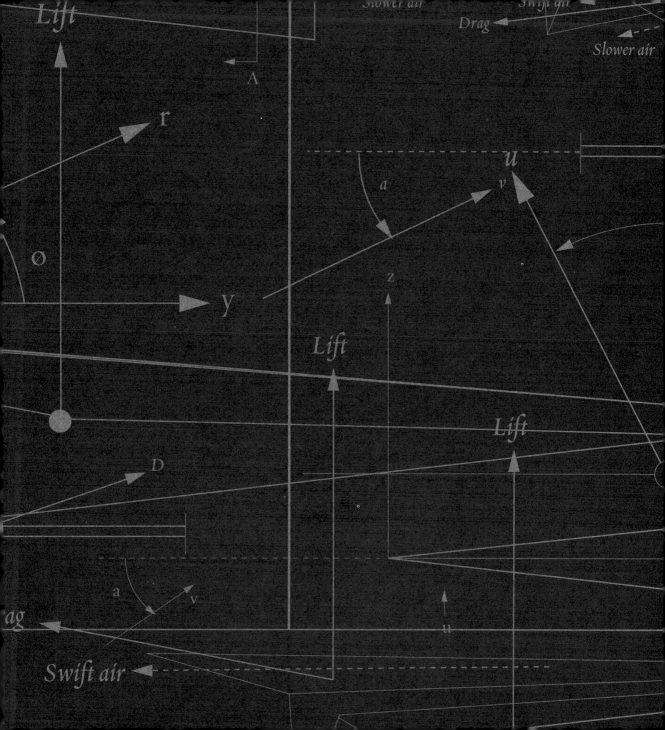

Simon & Schuster
Rockefeller Center
1230 Avenue of the Americas
New York, NY 10020

Copyright © 2001 by McMillan Associates
All rights reserved, including the right of reproduction
in whole or in part in any form.

First Simon & Schuster edition 2004
Published by arrangement with McMillan Media

SIMON & SCHUSTER and colophon are registered
trademarks of Simon & Schuster, Inc.

For information regarding special discounts for bulk
purchases, please contact Simon & Schuster Special Sales
at 1-800-456-6798 or business@simonandschuster.com

Manufactured in Singapore

1 3 5 7 9 10 8 6 4 2

Library of Congress Cataloging-in-Publication Data
is available.

ISBN 0-7432-5629-8

Produced by McMillan Associates
www.mcmillandesign.com

Writing and creative direction: Michael McMillan
www.michaelmcmillan.com

Design: Elizabeth Choi, Megan Kearney

Photography: Megan Kearney,
Michael McMillan, Charlie Westerman

Contributors: Caroline Bruce, Tom Doty, Frank Fochetta,
Alice McMillan, David Rosenthal, Lisa (Smith) Sanderson,
Southeast School, Will Wells, Walter Weintz

Special thanks to Anne for providing her knowledge and
understanding . . . Mark, Paul and Sara, whose diverse
views are valued and provide much insight.

Paper Airplane: A Lesson for Flying Outside the Box

Michael McMillan

Simon & Schuster

New York · London · Toronto · Sydney · Singapore

This story has little to do with the scien

In fact, the information about aerodynam.

It's more about vision, courage an

reality for his classmates, teacher

the Art of making paper airplanes.

flying is somewhat limited.

sixth grade boy's ability to change

nd maybe even those who read this book.

The intensity of the rush left me fighting to understand.

time stopped

11 . 10 . 9 . 8 . 7 . 6 . 5 . 4 . 3 . 2 . 1

It forced me

to keep that

precise moment

alive forever—

creating

an experience

that said:

"I was taken

Today, people call it thinking "out-of-the-box" or "paradigm-shift" thinking—

seeing something in an entirely different way.

Taking action on ideas to achieve breakthrough results sounds pretty good in theory. But experience teaches us the consequences of going against what is accepted—and believed to be correct. Even the best ideas can result in failure, often because of people's resistance to change. So why expend the energy—and risk failure—trying to change what's already "right"?

Throughout our lives, we are taught standard patterns of acceptable thinking. These patterns influence our laws, politics and religions. In short, they become our reality, our truth. So naturally, whenever they're challenged, and better results occur, the outcome can have a great impact. Ultimately, accepted practices give way to different forms of thinking, and another "right" way of doing things is born, causing us to readjust our thinking and adapt to a new reality.

"Open your books so we can review the section on aerodynamics. Once we're finished, we'll go outside and do an experiment that involves a contest.

Over the past week, we've studied many of man's attempts to fly. We've learned how two self-taught brothers made history on December 17, 1903, by being the first to sustain controlled, powered flight. While the flight lasted only 12 seconds, the plane they built managed to fly 120 feet.

What made the Wright brothers believe they could successfully build a machine that could fly when everyone else before them had failed, and often died trying?

Yes, Nancy?"

"Orville Wright studied everything he could about flying. He looked at how birds flew. He figured out that they moved the tips of their wings to keep their balance and steer. Oh, yeah. He also flew kites."

"Okay, good, Nancy. Orville realized that birds maintained lateral control by using the tips of their wings—something others had overlooked. And you're right, he used kites and gliders to test some of his thinking.

But, remember, the Wright Brothers found the accepted information on flying was wrong, so they had to establish their own. Their breakthrough thinking launched a new field of science and changed the way the world looked at flying."

"Yesterday, we discussed other
breakthroughs in flying. We learned about velocity,
weight and surface forces—drag, lift and thrust. Before we start
our experiment, remember what we learned about wing shapes? Wings are
engineered to cut through the air. The more streamlined the shape, the less resistance.
And less resistance results in faster planes that can travel farther."

"Okay, choose a flying partner."

"Hey Jeff,
  wanna be partners?"

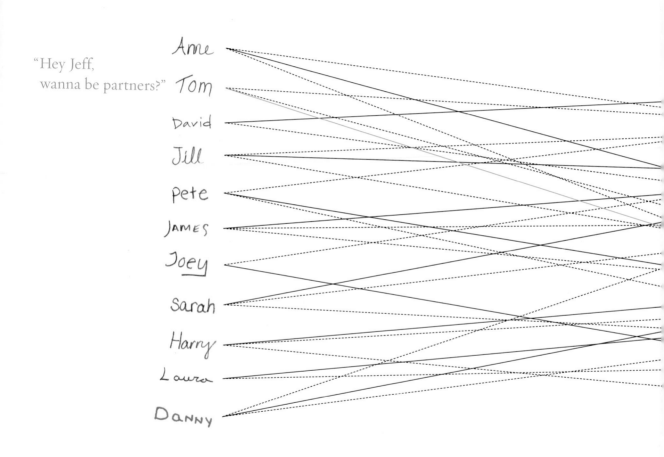

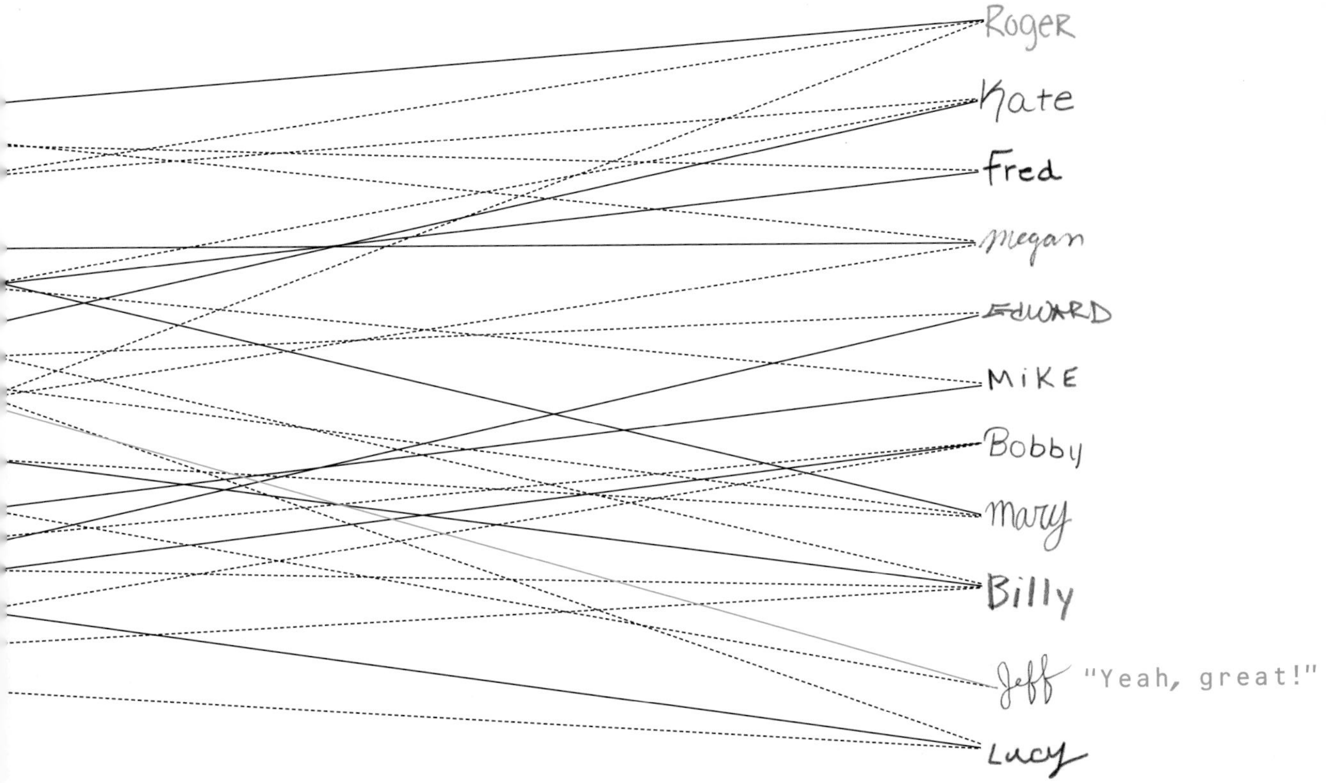

Roger

Kate

Fred

Megan

Edward

Mike

Bobby

Mary

Billy

Jeff   "Yeah, great!"

Lucy

| J | E | F | F | E | W | A | S | A | E | G | O | O | D | O | C | F | R | I | E | N | D |
|---|---|---|---|---|---|---|---|---|---|---|---|---|---|---|---|---|---|---|---|---|---|
| W | D | F | H | E | J | L | I | K | E | D | W | F | H | T | O | M | F | H | G | C | F |
| J | A | D | E | A | A | H | D | O | T | A | J | D | O | A | A | J | D | O | A | H | D |
| F | P | C | R | E | A | T | I | V | E | O | F | S | T | A | L | K | S | E | I | A | S |
| R | R | T | O | E | H | A | Q | Y | E | E | R | Q | Y | T | O | R | H | I | M | L | Q |
| C | L | V | E | A | I | Y | V | B | A | A | L | V | E | B | A | B | V | E | M | I | V |
| P | A | R | A | D | I | G | M | E | M | I | A | U | I | E | E | W | I | D | U | S | R |
| C | D | E | C | O | M | I | B | C | U | P | W | I | N | S | H | I | F | T | F | H | E |
| O | T | O | P | U | N | E | S | A | U | U | E | S | M | N | I | E | S | T | F | U | S |
| U | B | R | A | L | T | U | E | U | C | F | L | I | G | H | T | O | E | L | I | N | E |
| R | P | M | P | E | Q | J | O | S | E | A | P | R | Z | S | E | U | N | Z | N | W | R |
| A | U | S | E | K | U | U | H | E | A | L | W | A | Y | S | H | I | E | T | Y | S | S |
| G | E | S | E | E | M | E | D | I | H | B | E | Y | E | H | T | A | W | I | S | H | G |
| E | L | V | U | J | J | T | V | U | F | I | N | D | M | E | A | N | I | N | G | J | V |
| S | D | P | O | K | L | O | P | E | U | G | I | O | N | T | H | I | N | G | S | T | P |
| O | N | L | M | K | H | I | L | P | K | R | I | L | P | K | Q | H | D | P | Y | A | L |
| T | F | O | E | O | F | T | A | E | E | F | T | H | I | F | F | D | A | Y | F | F | A |
| S | S | I | W | C | S | S | I | H | C | C | S | I | N | Z | C | I | I | N | L | C | I |
| C | H | A | N | G | E | T | T | Q | R | R | O | E | Q | R | R | D | E | Q | R | A | E |
| A | C | T | I | O | N | O | E | A | O | P | E | O | P | L | E | N | E | A | O | O | N |
| E | E | S | A | I | R | P | L | A | N | E | E | S | F | O | U | T | H | W | D | N | S |

He was always coming up with things to make people laugh. Some people might say he was the class clown, but I didn't think of him that way.

He was really smart, but he didn't do so well in school.
I think he could have done well...

Actually, I'm not really sure. It's hard to tell.

He was a dreamer. It seemed like he always had something else on his mind—something that only he understood. So he rarely discussed the topic at hand, unless it was open for a new point of view.

He just seemed bored and restless like school held him back from discovering life's great secrets.

Jeff was an unusual kid. Better yet, he was unique.

At any given time, he could be staring out the window in deep thought, sharing a theory he had been pondering, making the class laugh, or challenging the relevance of our daily assignment.

Depending on whom you asked, Jeff was viewed as a smart kid who didn't apply himself, a dreamer who marched to a different beat, or in many cases, a kid who caused trouble by not following directions—challenging the status quo.

Good or bad, he was usually on some sort of mission. He didn't quit when he put his mind to something.

He liked making things happen—he liked winning.

That's the other reason I wanted him as my partner!

"Come up front and get a piece of construction paper."

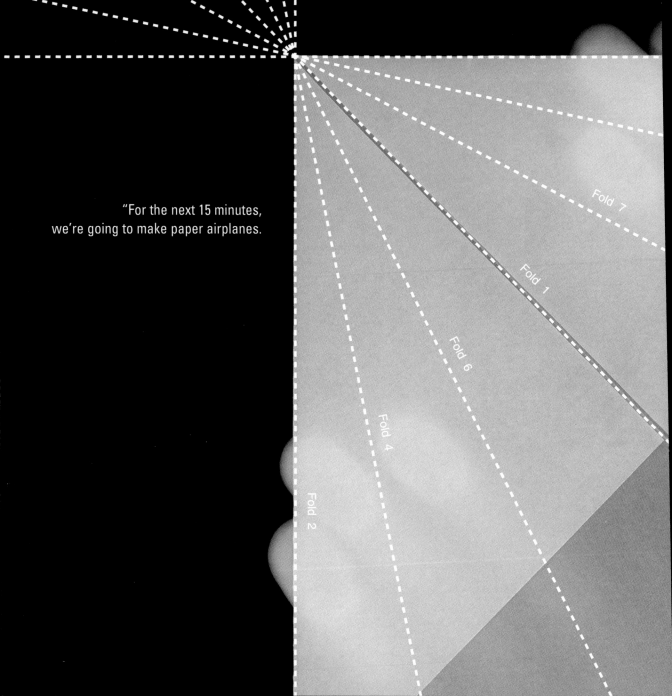

"For the next 15 minutes,
we're going to make paper airplanes.

Then we'll go outside and fly them."

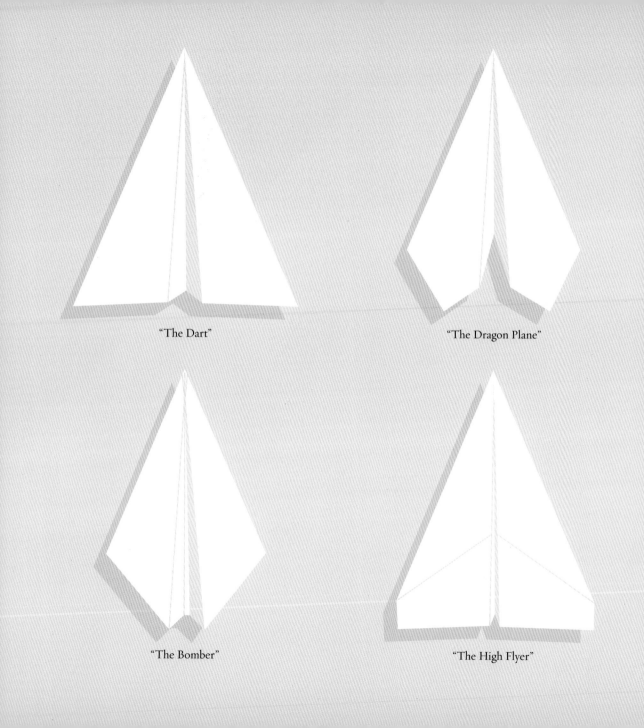

"The Dart"

"The Dragon Plane"

"The Bomber"

"The High Flyer"

"The Super Fighter"

"The Creeper"

"The Kite"

"The Magellan"

"Any questions?

Yes, Sara?"

"Can we color our planes?"

"Good question. Do you have enough time?
Will coloring make them go farther?"

"Jeff, what kind of plane are you gonna make?"

"Don't know yet," Jeff said in a state of deep thought.

"Well, I think I'm gonna do a regular kind of fold, except this tir

're gonna win. I can feel it." I tried to be a positive partner.

ı gonna make the sharpest point possible to cut through the air."

Ten minutes passed

I was all finished with my plane and had my popsicle stick marker ready to go.

Jeff was still thinking.

"Everyone line up with your partner. We're going to put your planes to the te

All of the planes looked pretty much the same.

Some were nicer than others.

One looked like a nosedive waiting to happen.

Another looked like it could fly for a mile if the wind was right.

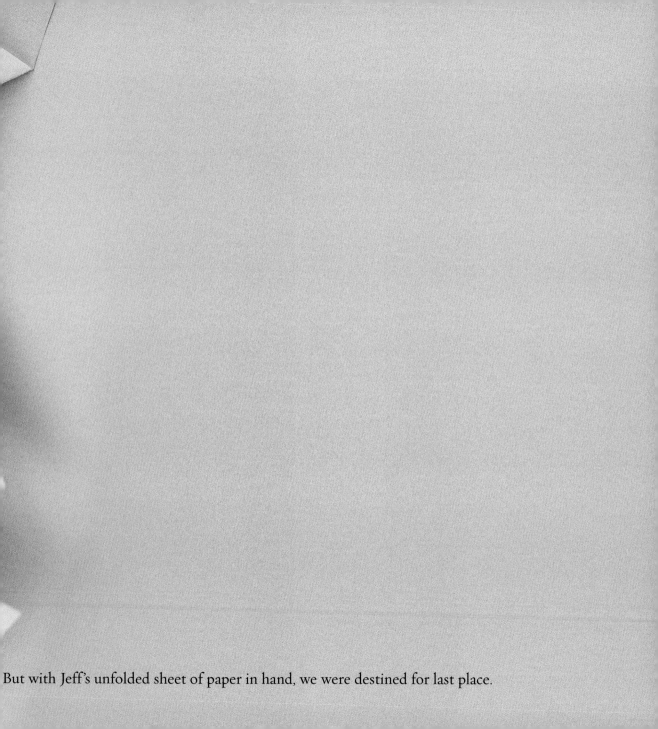

But with Jeff's unfolded sheet of paper in hand, we were destined for last place.

"Jeff, anything's better than nothing at all."

anyt

hing

Jeff still hadn't made a single crease in his paper.

I was really beginning to question my choice of partners.

"I'll ask Mrs. Hackett if we can go last...

Yes, she said it was okay. We're up last."

The experiment was interesting with many unexpected twists.

| Teams | Distance | | | |
|---|---|---|---|---|
| Team 1 | | ✖ | | |
| Team 2 | | | | |
| Team 3 | | | ✖ | |
| Team 4 | ✖ | | | |
| Team 5 | | ✖ | | ✖ |
| Team 6 | ✖ | | | |
| Team 7 | ✖ | | | |
| Team 8 | | | ✖ | |
| Team 9 | | | | |
| Team 10 | | | | |
| Team 11 | | | | |

Some planes barely flew five feet.

| | Combined Distance |
|---|---|
| | 13' 6" |
| | 29' 2" |
| | 24' 10" |
| | 13' 6" |
| | 11' 8" |
| | 14' 0" |
| | 16' 9" |
| Others did surprisingly well. | 25' 1" |
| | |
| | |
| | |

Everyone waited in anticipati

But one thing was certain: The line was thinning down...

Jeff was still holding a flat piece of construction paper

"Tom and Jeff, you're next."

"Just go, don't worry about me."

I walked up to the line as all my classmates watched. As smoothly as I could, I launched my plane.

Not too bad, better than average. If Jeff could only duplicate my distance, we'd be serious contenders.

Jeff approached the line with his craft well hidden behind his back.

Then he exposed his masterpiece—a flat, unviolated sheet of paper. With great confidence...

He wadded up the paper into a ball

and threw it farther than any of the leading planes had flown.          The crowd went...

NO FAIR!

CHEATER!!!

@#?!@#?

SOUT

Mr. L. L
Mrs. Ha

Nobody was certain how to feel or what to say, not even Mrs. Hackett.

We were all taken by the moment.

Jeff explained that to his way of thinking, by crumpling the paper into a ball, he could throw his plane with more force—kind of like a baseball. And because there was no wing interference—it was able to travel the greatest distance.

Jeff demonstrated a new way of interpreting a problem and had the courage to act on his vision.

My sixth-grade class would never be the same.

*Looking back in front of me*

While Jeff's paper airplane approach was new to his class, the concept of "breakthrough" ideas and "paradigm shifts"... or, whatever you choose to call it has been around since the beginning of time. Solving problems is at the foundation of our survival. There have always been people who thought differently, or did something in a new way. They're the ones responsible for nearly every subject taught today. Good or bad, the vision and determination of creative people have and will continue to impact our lives.

In a way, learning and finding breakthrough concepts can be viewed as a journey of sorts. However, on this journey, there's usually too little time to determine your own destination, much less the way you'll travel. Instead, you're handed a map with detailed instructions telling you where to go and how to get there. Maps simply explain the territory you've yet to explore. They're based on information and understanding gained by earlier travelers. While maps can be helpful, they can also be detrimental to creative thinking. If you follow them too closely, you can miss information not seen or understood by the map's creator.

Because most people prefer safe, predictable results, "proven" maps are usually handed out and followed closely. They are considered objective, therefore making them easier to teach and establish a standard against which to measure. Without realizing it, you're thinking inside-the-box. Jeff however, took a different path. He traveled through uncharted territory and found a new solution to a problem. And, in doing so, he risked experiencing undesirable results, viewed by most people as failure.

the potential of Jeff's plane always existed—it's just that nobody in the class had taken ~~the time~~ their eyes off the map they'd been handed. If they did, they either missed it or feared getting lost. They were just doing what they were taught—following the proven map, then showing how well they understood it by folding and flying their planes accordingly.

I've always found it interesting that throughout history nearly all people now recognized as brilliant mostly ignored the maps they were given. And contrary to what's typically explained, it's not because they mastered the proven maps first and then moved on. It's because they didn't understand or accept them, so they created their own.

The map Jeff's teacher provided was based on solid aviation information developed by intelligent people dedicated to finding new answers. It was a good map. However, it dealt more with engine-powered airplanes— not paper ones. Sometimes a good map is applied to the wrong territory. When this happens, you can get more lost than if you had no map at all. I think most maps are originally created with solid intentions—whether it's getting from (A) to (B) or whatever. It's just that over time unrelated information and agendas are slowly added to them. When people spend (too much) time and energy focusing on the wrong issues, and once again, thinking inside-the-box appears

If people are respectfully allowed to think, grow and contribute with their individual abilities, we will learn much faster about the unseen truths that surround us each day. By letting people create their own maps, we will build momentum for discovery and achieve more profound insight and understanding.

Perhaps this story will serve as an idea map — challenged by everyone who reads it. Hopefully, it will be improved or replaced by someone more capable of seeing things I missed along the way, on my journey. I don't have all the answers... No one does. Maybe that's a good starting point when we think about important things like raising children, establishing educational programs, building businesses — leading fulfilling lives.

Have you ever thougHT tHere'd bE a day when peoplE thiNk a Different way?
And on that day, what would you say, if you still thought the other way?

—*Paul McMillan*

*Written in the 8th grade*

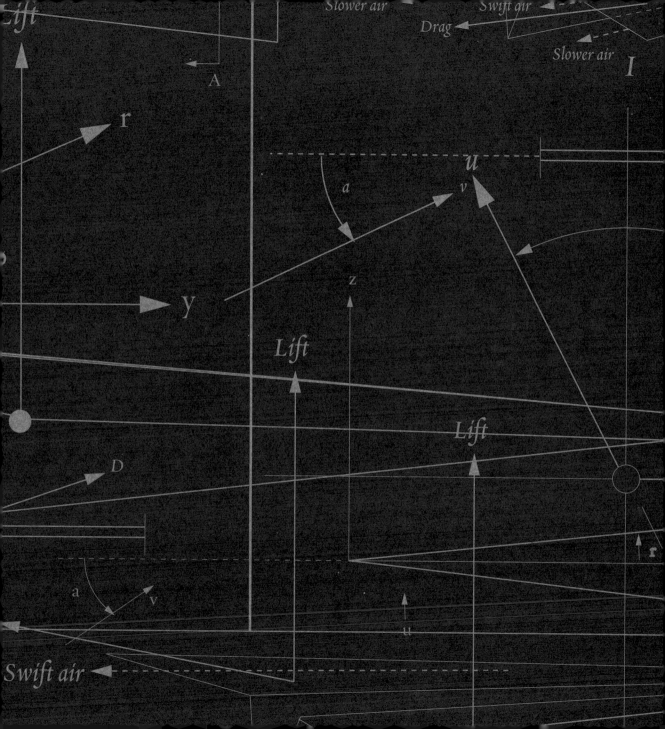

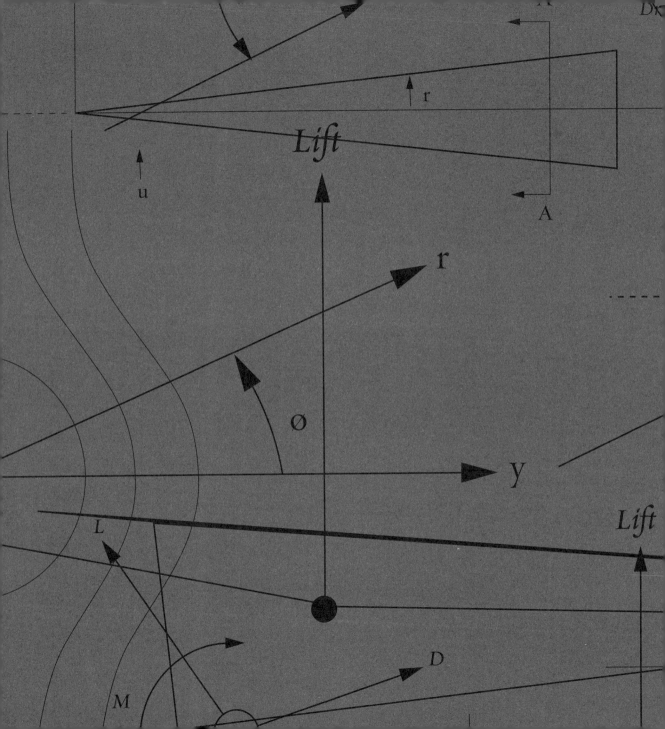